Shopify:
Beginner to Pro Guide – The Comprehensive Guide

(Shopify, Shopify Pro, Shopify Store, Shopify Dropshipping, Shopify Beginners Guide)

By Timothy Short

Table of Contents

Introduction – 8
Chapter 1: How Shopify Works - 10
Chapter 2: Decide What to Sell - 17
Chapter 3: Sourcing Products - 26
Chapter 4: Getting Started - 34
Chapter 5: Marketing - 43
Chapter 6: Expanding Your Product Line - 55
Conclusion - 59

© Copyright 2016 by DCB Web Trading Ltd__ All rights reserved.

This document is presented with the desire to provide reliable, quality information about the topic in question and the facts discussed within. This eBook is sold under the assumption that neither the author nor the publisher should be asked to provide the services discussed within. If any discussion, professional or legal, is otherwise required a proper professional should be consulted.

This Declaration was held acceptable and equally approved by the Committee of Publishers and Associations as well as the American Bar Association.

The reproduction, duplication or transmission of any of the included information is considered illegal whether done in print or electronically. Creating a recorded copy or a secondary copy of this work is also prohibited unless the action of doing so is first cleared through the Publisher and condoned in writing. All rights reserved.

Any information contained in the following pages is considered accurate and truthful and that any liability through inattention or by any use or misuse of the topics discussed within falls solely on the reader. There are no cases in which the Publisher of this work can be held responsible or be asked to provide reparations for any loss of monetary gain or other damages which may be caused by following the presented information in any way shape or form.

The following information is presented purely for informative purposes and is therefore considered universal. The information presented within is done so without a contract or any other type of assurance as to its quality or validity.

Any trademarks which are used are done so without consent and any use of the same does not imply consent or permission was gained from the owner. Any trademarks or brands found within are purely used for clarification purposes and no owners are in anyway affiliated with this work.

Introduction

Congratulations on purchashing *Shopify: Beginner to Pro Seller – The Comprehensive Guide* and thank you for doing so. Starting your own online store is a major decision whether you are interested in building an active or a passive income stream and purchasing this book is a great step in the right direction. It is also the easiest step as setting up your own successful online store will require plenty of hard work and determination but that's not to say it won't be fun!

It is more than doable and the following chapters will discuss just how you can go about making your dream of an online store a reality. Inside you will learn all about the specifics of the Shopify platform and what makes it the best choice when it comes to starting your online store. You will also find tips related to choosing the products to sell that are right for you, getting your site up and running and marketing it properly. Finally, it ends with a look to the future and how you will know when to expand your product line.

There are plenty of books on this subject on the market, thanks again for choosing this one! Every effort was made to ensure it is full of as much useful information as possible so you'll never have to buy another book on this subject again. Please enjoy!

Chapter 1: How Shopify Works

When it comes to starting a successful online business the online sales and marketing platform that you use can be either the flagship of your entire launch or the anchor around your new online store's neck. The right choice for many individuals and the one you are likely going to be the most satisfied with in the long run is Shopify.com. For nearly 2 decades Shopify has been providing ecommerce solutions for small business who want to take their business online.

Shopify is what is known as a complete ecommerce solution for business that are looking to sell their products online. The site will allow you to create a personalized online store, sell any products that you like and also accept payments from debit and credit cards while also tracking orders and providing customer service. When it comes to creating an online home for your store, there are many web building platforms and online payment solutions to choose from, Shopify takes all the hassle out of mixing and matching and puts all the tools for getting your online business up and running successfully in one place.

Shopify is more than a simple marketplace where goods are exchanged, it is also what is known as a payment gateway which means it handles the transaction verification process required to ensure that those who pay for your goods via debit or credit card actually have the funds to complete the purchase. It also means they are responsible for the security concerns related to these transactions which can be both complicated and expensive for merchants to pursue themselves.

When it comes to deciding how you want to use Shopify, the first thing you will need to determine is if you want to create your own site and then link it Shopify or if you are more interested in getting started as quickly, easily and cheaply as possible by using the store that Shopify will provide at all levels of service. While the option to create your own site will certainly cost more, it will give you complete control over the customer experience which is an important consideration if the niche you are considering working with is extremely competitive.

Payment plans
After a 2-week trial, Shopify users are asked to pick the usage plan that is right for them. The various tiers allow for different levels of features as well as differing number of items you can list for sale.

Starter: The basic tier of Shopify service is $14 per month and includes the ability to list 25 items for sale. This is the perfect option for those who are just getting a feel for online sales and don't want to be able to do too much too soon.

Basic: At twice the cost of the starter option, the basic tier of service allows an unlimited number of items to be listed for sale. It also offers telephone support, 1 gigabyte of storage, a waiver of all transaction fees, unlimited bandwidth usage and a credit card charge rate of 2.9 percent plus an additional 30 cents per each transaction made. If you are thinking about creating a company that dropships items, then this is the service tier you are likely going to want to consider.

Professional: For an additional $50 each month, professional tier users are allotted 5 gigabytes of store storage space which allows for high resolution photographs for products that require a greater degree of visible detail. Additionally, you will be able to offer gift cards to your users as well as recover their old shopping carts. You will also be privy to an improved credit and debit card transaction rate of 2.5 percent plus 30 cents per charge. Perhaps most importantly, this tier of service provides access to an advanced suite of analytics tools to more accurately monitor customer behavior.

Unlimited: The unlimited Shopify plan offers no limits on the amounts of data that your store uses for the cost of $179 each month. This option is only really needed by professional businesses who are using carrier shipping and need real time results. It offers a credit and debit card transaction rate of 2.25 percent as well as the 30 cents per transaction fee.

Expectations
When you start off with a basic Shopify site you can expect something akin to a basic WordPress site but without any of the related plugins. This niche can be filled on the Shopify application store which offers numerous varieties of applications for either no charge, or a one-time or monthly usage fee. Many of the most common and useful applications are available free of charge and it is simply up to you to determine which ones are going to be right for you. More information on important applications can be found in chapter 4.

Likewise, when first starting off it is important to have a realistic understanding of how much space you will need for the pictures of the products you are going to be selling and budget accordingly. For new businesses, it is unlikely you will need more than 1 gigabyte of allotted space before you start looking to expand your product line as discussed in chapter 6. Shopify offers up numerous options when it comes to website creation but it is also possible to use any of the major CMS platforms including WordPress, Joomla or Drupal to create a more unique looking site, though you will need to code, or pay someone to code, the site in such a way that it plays nice with Shopify.

If you are not able to supply the coding knowledge yourself it is important to budget at least $2,000 for this project, with many more elaborate jobs easily doubly or tripling this rate. If you are going down this route it is important to have a very clear idea of what you want the end result to be as any changes are going to cost you dearly. To get a better idea of what all you are going to need to have in mind to create your brand successfully, check out chapter 5.

Remember, if you choose to only be connected to the Shopify network but not take advantage of their all in one service you will need to individually source all of the elements of your site including the site itself as well as any hosting and credit card transaction fees. The costs and hassles of working with several different companies adds up quickly, which makes the basic Shopify solution the most cost effective and easiest choice for many new online business owners to make.

When it comes to payment solutions you will have the option of using Shopify Payments which will be built into your store and is powered by Stripe technology. If you don't like the sound of the rates outlined above, then you are free to look into a third party transaction verification service which will be a more convoluted process that will ultimately save those who use it time and money in the long run. Additionally, it is important to note that Shopify payments are not available in all regions as well.

The biggest downside for many of these third party programs is that users are required to have a merchant account in order to qualify which can be a difficult process for small businesses who are already processing a fair amount of transactions but may not have the best overall credit history. Acquiring a merchant account is a complicated process which requires a detailed history of previous successful transactions your online business has conducted as well as proof of a successful business plan. Merchant accounts are given out by debit and credit card companies and they are anxious to ensure that the transactions they verify are going to go through on the merchant level as well as the consumer one as they are the ones on the hook if it all falls apart.

Additional features
Assuming you decide to create your site through Shopify directly you will find that you immediately have access to a wide range of free templates, each with a number of variations and every one designed with a specific type of store in mind. Each of the basic templates are all also guaranteed to be responsive which means you will not have to worry about designs not translating to mobile platforms. There are also numerous paid templates that typically range between $100 and $300, though if you are planning on paying for a template you will

likely want to pay a little more and have one created for you from scratch for the best results.

As long as you choose the basic level of service or above you will also have access to the ability to sell both physical and digital goods and charge any shipping rate of your choice as well as PayPal integration for even more payment options. You will also be able to start a blog and send email blasts, the importance of both is emphasized in chapter 5, as well as add a buy now button to any existing websites. Additionally, you will have the ability to create staff accounts, discount codes and have access to additional point-of-sale integration options.

For those who own small physical businesses and are interested in taking them online, perhaps the most important Shopify functionality is its point-of-sale kit which lets them make the most of their Shopify accounts by using it to process payments in the real world as well with the help from any Android or iOS device as long as they are in Canada or the United States. The point of sale kit includes everything a small business holder would need to take credit and debit card payments including a receipt printer, barcode scanner, card reader and even a cash drawer. It also works with pieces of existing systems.

Chapter 2: Decide What to Sell

When it comes to creating an online store on Shopify, the first thing you are going to want to do is figure out just what it is you want to sell. Finally settling on the right product for you is immensely vital to the ultimate long term success or failure of your store which means it should not be taken lightly. In addition to determining your profit margins, it will determine what type of marketing options are available to you which is why you should aim to find a product that fills a need in a niche that is competitive but not over full. Finding just the right mix of scarcity and demand can be difficult, but you will know it when you see it.

Focus on the demand
When it comes to finding the right items to sell, the first thing you should look for are different groups of individuals who all share a variety of similar traits. This is called a niche and finding the right one is first step to determining what you are going to sell. When it comes to targeting the right niche you are going to want to find one that has a fair amount of disposable income, and ideally, a hobby or interest that comes with the need to purchase lots of accessories or equipment as well. While this may sound easy, many of the obvious niches are already extremely competitive which is why it may take some thinking to find the right niche for you.

Once you find a niche that you think is not extremely competitive, the next thing you will want to determine is if there is enough of a demand for specific products in the niche in question. A market could be underserved because you got to it first, or it could be underserved because there isn't enough demand to justify the time and effort required to sell the products in question. To determine which it is, start by making a list of items that you expect to eventually sell to the niche audience in question and then take some time to search for each of them via Google.

As you are typing in each product, be on the lookout for the items that autofill into the list of suggestions as this is a great indicator of want or need in a given niche. Specifically, you want to keep an eye out for searches that indicate an unmet need when it comes to the products in question including questions about where to find or who sells the product in question. Additionally, you can find out more when it comes to unmet needs by performing the same search engine query on sites like Etsy and eBay.

Check on the competition
Once you have an idea of what items are in need in the niche, your next step should be to determine the level of competition when it comes to a specific item types. The more online stores that you find selling the same product or variations thereon the more direct competition you will have when it comes time to actually start selling products. I you can find more than 2 pages of search results selling the items you are thinking about selling with no more than a basic search you may want to consider a different niche or at least targeting a sub-niche to carve out more of a unique audience.

While checking out the competition you will want to do all of the reconnaissance to ensure that you have a good idea of what their product turnover seems to be and how robust their customer base seems to be. While scouting out the competition it is important to approach them in a rational fashion and not set out determined to crush them no matter what. At this point is likely a better choice to cut your losses and find another niche before you start putting real time and effort into this one; remember, discretion is the better part of valor.

Additionally, you will want to consider the strength of any obvious competitor's social media campaigns and search engine optimization SEO. To determine how popular and effective each is, you simply need to do basic searches with terms related to the niche you are interested in infiltrating. If a few names keep coming up again and again and again, then you may want to consider looking for a new product to sell.

Determine if anything is going to set you apart from the pack
Depending on what you find during your initial fact finding mission your next step will need to be figuring out just what is going to set you and your products apart from all of the other stores that are offering similar, if not the same product. What this typically comes down to is how much personality or added value you can add to your store, to the point that it makes it preferable for customers to seek you out instead of simply jumping on Amazon for the purchase and calling it a day.

This means you will likely need to factor in additional costs, whether it is for additional items that are given away for free as incentives for single or multiple sales, or for the additional costs that will likely be accrued from creating a more personalized and unique website. If you are interested in creating a brand instead of simply selling items in an online store, then your best bet when it comes to choosing items to sell is likely going to related to a niche that you consider yourself an expert in. Generating additional content is a great way to get potential customers to your site before hopefully coercing them into a sale and having the knowledge beforehand can make content generation much easier. If you aren't sure what to do about

Put quality first
Once you have an idea of what types of items you are interested in selling, you will likely be tempted to start sourcing them from the cheapest vendor possible to ensure maximum profit as soon as possible. It is important to resist this urge, however, as a focus on quality will go a long way towards setting yourself apart from the pack. Especially early on when you have no other reputation to speak of, a few reviews indicating a subpar quality can be the kiss of death for a new online business. Instead of looking for the cheapest products possible, it is important to instead look for the highest quality products you can find and chalk up the difference to an early and especially effective form of marketing.

Physical products
When it comes to selling items on Shopify, physical goods still outnumber digital goods to a significant degree. Though much of this market is controlled by global brands, the percentage of this trillion-dollar market that small business is expected to control is estimated to be on the rise and may grow by more than 40 percent in the next 5 years.

Pros

- Psychologically, many people, especially those of older generations, are simply more comfortable paying for physical as opposed to digital goods which means that every physical goods deal will be easier to sell, at least for now.

- Physical products are also still unilaterally trusted more than their digital counterparts. Many of the stigmas from early days of the internet remain, including that downloaded products are more likely to work incorrectly than their physical counterparts.

- If you decide to sell physical products, you will have access to a much wider variety of products as well as distributors of products to choose from.

Cons

- Physical products are always going to incur costs at every step of the way, production costs, shipping costs, storage costs and generally another round of shipping costs are all often required. This typically results in a lower profit margin as well.

- Some physical products cannot be shipped to certain areas and other items cannot be shipped at all due to their delicate nature. All the concerns related to an item's sheer physicality are all on this list as well.

Digital products

A majority of digital products that are sold on Shopify fall into the information category. This includes things likes movies, music, books, patterns, templates and more. Digital products are selling more and more every year and eBooks have actually been selling more copies than physical books since 2012.

Pros

- Digital content can be created more easily than many physical object which limits costs significantly, specifically when it comes to manufacturing or costs related to storage.

- Shipping costs are also not a concern because digital items can be sent electronically and customers can be using their products minutes after purchasing them.

- These other benefits combine to create much higher profit margins on average when it comes to digital as opposed to physical items, even though the physical items typical cost much more.

Cons

- Piracy poses a significant threat to all types of digital content as once it has been pirated its value drops to practically 0 in nearly all instances.

- The digital quality of more complicated digital files is limited by the common use infrastructure that limits the size of practical files.

- Certain items simply cannot have a digital analog which makes the digital market inherently limited to a few specific fields.

- The current quality limitations of technology ensure that physical copies of media will currently always look or sound better than digital alternatives.

Subscription Products
One of the more recent ecommerce trends, if you use your Shopify account to sell a subscription service then you are getting people to promise to pay you a set amount each month in exchange for a predetermined level of products that are automatically sent out at a specific period of time. The items are niche specific, but generally the exact makeup of each monthly purchase is determined by the seller which means a subscription model can be quite profitable when utilized properly.

Pros

- Subscription boxes automatically generate customer loyalty by forcing customers to commit to an implied long term relationship right up front.

- It can be easy to build an initial customer base as it is easy for customers to buy in at the promise of trying something new.

- Complete brand control over an entire product line.

- Great choice for products that naturally wear out somewhat quickly after regular use.

Cons

- Regardless of the items in question, subscriptions are often seen as luxury items which means they are the first things cut during financial crisis.

- Ensuring that reoccurring billing is correct can be extremely difficult as customers often won't think of such services until the payment has already failed to go through.

- If the cost from the supplier changes unexpectedly you are still on the hook for the agreed upon amount.

Chapter 3: Sourcing Products

Once you have a clear idea of the type of products you are interested in selling, the next step is to figure out where you are going to get your products from.

Wholesalers
When it comes to sourcing items for an online store, the most common option that many people think of is seeking out a wholesaler to purchase the products from before reselling them to the public. If you are interested in wholesaling the first thing you will need to determine is if you are going to look for local retailers or deal with a wholesaler abroad. While prices will always be cheaper overseas, the biggest determining factor is often what type of items you are interested in selling. There are many items that can simply not be shipped internationally due to complicated regulations and the importing process can quickly become laborious in these cases. Likewise, the international shipping process is nowhere near as gentle on packages so many fragile items will likely need to be sourced locally as well.

In these instances, you will most likely want to avoid seeking out wholesalers online, as many of these sites are more middlemen than true wholesalers which means the best prices can be found elsewhere. Specifically, they can be found at wholesaler tradeshows which are surprisingly common once you start looking for them. The vendors you meet in these instances will be those who can actually create the kind of deals that you are looking for; and what's more, the tradeshow environment means that every vendor is eager to make deals to make a sale to ensure the expenses and hassle of the trade show are recouped in new business.

Alternatively, if you are looking for the best prices, bar none, and you are looking for the types of products that can be shipped internationally, then the Asian wholesale market is likely going to be your best bet. For a good idea of where to start, check Alibaba.com and look for the companies that these online stores are getting their products from.

When dealing with foreign vendors, it is important to communicate via email instead of over the phone as the language barrier will be less pronounced this way. Additionally, this way you will get everything that is agreed to in writing, which will be beneficial as these types of contracts are likely to be more fluid than many of the contracts you are used to. What's more, you will likely want to add some additional time to your roll out plan to ensure you can receive multiple defective batches of products before finding an acceptable quality, just in case. Remember, forewarned is forearmed.

Dropshipping
Depending on the products you are thinking about selling, you might not actually need to source inventory at all. Certain types of products are frequently sold through a type of fulfillment transaction that is referred to as dropshipping. In this relationship, you, as the merchant, would sell items on your Shopify page and then leave the procurement, storage, and shipping of the item to a third-party company who will then take a portion of the profits for their time and trouble.

Dropshipping is great for those who are anxious to get started selling items via Shopify as quickly as possible as it means they can get started with practically no setup time or startup costs. The downside of dropshipping includes that you are limited to the types of products you can sell as they must be carried by your dropshipping company while also being limited in most cases to local fulfillment companies. Additionally, you will always make less of a profit when it comes to dropshipping, though the process will be more passive than if you procured your own stock.

When it comes to choosing a dropshipping company to work with, it is important to take the time to really do your homework on the companies you are considering. As a merchant whose supply is solely dependent on others, you are going to want to ensure that your vendor is as reliable as humanly possible, both in terms of delivering packages in a prompt fashion and in terms of their own supply chain. As a merchant, there is nothing worse than not being able to get in touch with your dropshipping company, and as long as you do your research you can easily avoid this fate.

You will also want to take the time to determine what the process for handling customer returns is like as you are still going to be the point of contact for any customer service questions your customers might have. Taking the time to find a dropshipping company with a streamlined customer returns process can literally save you hours of time in the long run, avoid looking into it at your own peril.

Private Label
A private label product is any product that is manufactured by someone else and then sold and branded by you for sale exclusively on your Shopify page. As the merchant and owner of the brand in question you are able to determine exactly what the product is going to look like, what it will be made out of and even what the packaging looks like. Private label products won't work for every niche, and the initial cost is always going to be much higher; if your private label brand takes off, however, then you stand to make significantly more from your Shopify page than you otherwise might.

Consumer products that traditionally have private labels includes things like frozen foods, dairy products, salad dressings, condiments, household cleaning products, paper goods, cosmetic, beverages and personal care or beauty products. While quite common in grocery stores, the practice of creating private label goods is seen less often in online stores where the idea of coming across a product brand you have never heard of before is much less unusual.

The advantages of creating a branded product line up with all of the things you are going to be interested in as a new merchant including selling quality products, building your brand, controlling your pricing, building customer loyalty and spreading the word about your store with every product sold. Additionally, you will have the ability to expand more easily as you do not have to worry about finding new vendors for new products if you are making them yourself. Finally, you will always have a clear idea of what your profit margin is going to be because you have the final say on every aspect of the product which means there will never be any hidden charges or unexpected fees.

When it comes to limiting factors of creating your own products, the biggest is going to be cost. If dropshipping is the cheapest and easiest way of starting an online store, creating an entire product line is likely going to be the most complicated. First and foremost, you are going to need to do your homework, and lots of it, you are going to need to learn everything you can about the products you hope to sell, specifically what qualities the best versions contain as well as the types of materials or products they contain. With that out of the way you are going to need to compare manufacturers, which in and of itself is going to be a difficult process, further complicated by any limiting factors related to the products you are hoping to create.

Once you have gone through the prototyping phase for the product itself, you will need to do the same for the label and packaging for the product and hiring someone to help you through this process will cost around $100 per hour. Then you will need to worry about sourcing the materials you will want to use in large quantities if the private label company doesn't concern itself with such things. This is all before you even get to the actual production phase which means you are likely always going to be tied to the manufacturer in question, so you will need to ensure they are reliable and trustworthy. Finally, depending on the type of products being sold, many private label brands have a hard time building the type of following that more traditional brands are able to achieve.

Creating your own products
Depending on the types of products you will be selling, you may be able to forgo any type of more traditional manufacturing scenario and instead simply create everything you are going to sell by yourself. There are three different types of manufacturing that you can consider, the first is known as made to stock, which is where you crate the products beforehand and then use your Shopify page as a type of digital showroom.

To ensure you don't overspend on supplies in this scenario it is important to have a clear idea of what the expected demand for your product is going to be. Producing more of a product than you need tends to promote a sale mentality which can severely affect your bottom line depending on the amount of overestimation that occurred. Alternatively, you do not want to underestimate the demand that your product might receive as having too little stock on hand if your shop becomes popular early on can severely curtail your earnings potential in both the short or long term.

Another type of manufacturing strategy is to advertise the fact that your products are made to order based on customer specifications. This type of manufacturing ensures a natural inventory control mechanism and ensure you do not need to worry too much about the demand in the short term, as long as there is a steady stream of work coming in. Unfortunately, this type of manufacturing strategy won't work for every product category as the level of personalization possible will not equal out to the amount of extra time the order is going to take to create. If you hope to make this type of manufacturing work for you, you will need to ensure the added time comes with an appropriate amount of added value.

Finally, a combination of the above manufacturing strategies can be useful in many cases. This is what is known as made to assemble manufacturing and it would involve you completing as much of the manufacturing as possible prior to the point that customization is added. This method of manufacturing allows you to hedge your bets when it comes to market demand while also minimizing the amount of time required to create more personalized, and therefore sought after, items.

When it comes to creating your own items successfully, your goal at every turn should be to minimize as much risk as possible. If you have too much of a supply your demand will drop and if you don't supply enough then you might not be able to recoup your costs. As such, the most important thing to do is come up with a realistic business plan and stick to it no matter what.

Chapter 4: Getting Started

Once you have figured out what products your Shopify store is going to sell and where those products are going to come from, you are nearly finished getting your Shopify page sale ready.

Setting up a Shopify Store

1. *Make an account:* The first thing you will want to do is to go to Shopify.com and click on the Get Started button in the middle of the screen. This will get you set up with a 14-day free trial so you won't need to worry about choosing a service plan until that period has expired. You will be asked to enter a number of details before being given the opportunity to choose a store name. The name of your store will need to be unique and you will be prompted to choose another if your desired name is taken.

   You will then be asked for some additional personal information including contact and location information. You will also be asked about the status of your products in the section regarding what you will be selling. Choosing the I'm Done option will save your information and deposit you into the general Admin Screen.

2. *Personalize your page:* From the admin screen you can personalize you page by selecting a theme and adding applications that can do a wide variety of useful and interesting things. You also have the

opportunity to change the font used in a selected theme, as well as changing the color scheme, the layout of the page, adding additional item functionality and adding a number of rotating slides.

3. *Add products:* Once you have personalized your Shopify page as you see fit, you will want to start adding in the items that you want to sell. From the admin screen you can choose the Products button followed by the option to Add a product. The resulting screen will allow you to add a wide variety of information about your product and you should make it a point to include as many details about each product as possible as the more information your customers have available the more likely they are to find the product they are looking for. The description, name and unique and specific URL are all extremely important to maximize your SEO.

This is also the screen where you will be able to upload pictures of the items that you plan on selling. Pictures can be rearranged after they have been uploaded, so order isn't specific at this point; eventually, however, you will want to ensure that the first picture of all of your products is of someone interacting with the product in question. This will force your customers to picture themselves using the product which has been shown to increase conversion rates overall.

Additionally, you will want to include

pictures that provide the buyer a clear idea of what to expect when they receive the idea. All of your pictures should be of a high quality and contain a unified look, size and background. Finally, you will always want to select the Save Product button to save your new product.

4. *Create collections:* Collections are groups of related items that make it easy for customers to browse related items. Each product can appear in multiple collections simultaneously and each collection should appear on your Shopify landing page as well as in a section of your navigation bar. The collection screen can be found from the admin screen and works in much the same way the add product screen works. Once you fill out the relevant categories you can either have products that match the specifications listed automatically, or add items to collections by hand.

5. *Determine payment options:* On the admin screen, you will also be able to determine what types of payment options you are going to accept from customers. While the various rates and fees involved are important, it is equally important to make a concentrated effort to allow customers to give you money in as many ways as possible. The options for accepting payments via Shopify directly and via PayPal are automatically made available to you with additional options being presented as needed.

Those who live in either the United Kingdom or the United States will be connected with a Shopify payments account, to activate it all that needs to be done is go to the Settings option, followed by Payments and the Complete Shopify Payment account option. From there it is simply a matter of following the onscreen instructions.

6. *Related sales options:* If your items are going to require either taxes or shipping costs to be paid by the customer, you are going to want to ensure these are being displayed properly. To do so, visit the product page from the admin screen and then choose the options for Variants and Inventory. You will want to edit the Product Variant option and then the individual options for shipping or taxes respectively. When it comes to determining shipping costs, having an exact idea of the weight of each item is required.

7. *Maximize your SEO:* From the admin screen you will also want to check out the General tab which is where you can set things such as the title for your homepage as well as the meta details that you will want to include. Including the right meta data is crucial to helping prospective customers find your store and you should take the time to research the best description ideas for your niche in particular. This is also the screen that you use to list your physical business address if you have one.

8. *Set up shipping:* Shopify has numerous shipping options, but they are limited by what you choose to offer. To ensure you don't

miss out on sales due to lack of shipping options, select Shipping from the admin screen and then select the options that are right for you.

9. *Add a domain:* Without an actual domain name for your store, your Shopify page won't actually be able to reach anyone. You can use any hosting site that you like, or buy a domain name directly from Shopify for the cost of around $10 per year. Once you have decided on a domain, you will want to choose Settings from the admin screen before selecting the option for Domains. From there you will want to select the Add Existing Domain and after you enter in your Shopify domain the setup process should proceed automatically.

10. *Add a blog:* Shopify comes with built in blog content options for those who are interested in being seen as an expert in a particular field. To create a blog section of your sight simply choose the Blog Posts option from the admin page and create a new blog. Ensure you use the Pages option from the same screen to ensure that your blogs have a page of their own to live in on your site.

Protect yourself
When starting an online business, most people forget to treat it as they would any other business and then find themselves getting burned later on down the line. To prevent this from happening, it is in your best effort to create an LLC and do everything required of you to ensure your business when it comes to paying your taxes.

These days, creating a limited liability company is as easy as going to LegalZoom.com and choosing the signup option that is right for you. This is important as once you have created a corporation, you will not be able to be personally sued by any customers should something go horribly wrong in the future. An LLC limits your personal liability in these instances and ensures that the worst thing that can happen is that you have to shutter the business and move on.

The laws for collecting sales taxes vary by region which means that the first thing you will need to do is determine the law as it pertains to the area you are running the store in. In general, you will need to collect a sales tax from other individuals who are in your same state. Additionally, you will want to keep detailed records of all of your transactions so you have a clear idea of what you will need to pay on your personal income taxes next year. If you are unsure of what the tax requirements are for your store, speaking with a local professional who is familiar with the details of online sales is recommended.

Create a site with lots of conversions
Getting your Shopify store up and running is nice, building a store that ensures you conversion rate is as high as possible is another. Oftentimes, improving conversion rates are simply a matter of tweaking a few minor site choices, take a look at the following to ensure you are creating as compelling of sales scenario as possible.

Try A/B tests: A/B tests are a type of test you should do whenever you are unsure about some facet of your site. You will need an application to utilize it fully but essentially what you do is create 2 different pages which the application will then split your incoming customers to. You will then be able to quickly and easily see which of the two options is the better choice, not by going with your gut but by relying on the facts. When it comes to running A/B tests, you should always run them when it comes to determining your most successful landing page as well as the offers you are currently running in an effort to build customers. When first starting out it is also a good idea to test things like button sizes and the approach you use to getting people to sign up for your email newsletter.

Have a clear proposition for value: At its most basic, your conversion rate is primarily going to be determined by how compelling your value proposition really is. Your value proposition can be thought of as the main reason that customer will choose your product over those of the competitor. When determining your value proposition, start by asking yourself what the customer will think is in it for them if they buy your product. Once you have figured this out, try and determine how customers would determine this proposition from the very first page of your site. If your landing page doesn't make it clear what your value proposition is, you will lose out on sales, guaranteed.

A good value proposition is one that is clearly different from the value proposition of any of your competitors this means there must be one facet of your offer that is unique to your store and no one else's. Take your time when it comes to determining what your value proposition is, rushing to conclusions won't actually help anyone. You need to work on your value proposition until it can be clearly elucidated in a single sentence.

Create a funnel for sales: One of the major reasons that new online businesses have low conversion rates is that you are simply asking for the sale too quickly. To ensure that your customers are in the mood to buy something by the time they are presented with the option you need to create a way to move them through the decision to purchase the product in question.

The first step to doing so is understanding that the more expensive or cumbersome a product is; the more time the customer is going to need to mentally prepare themselves for the sale. If you are selling a digital product then this is as simple as offering a free trial, otherwise you need to start out by building awareness of the problem the product solves, before moving on to why your product is the best way to solve a specific problem and finally, why buying the product today is the best choice.

Chapter 5: Marketing

Once your Shopify page is up and running all that is left to do now is to market it like crazy to ensure that you grow your brand as quickly and steadily as possible.

Find your target audience
When you found the products you are now selling, you committed to a niche of the population that is interested in that product. The next step is to segment that niche down even further and determine just who you are likely going to sell the most products too. The easiest way to go about doing so is to first collect some information on customers who have purchased products from your store so far which means you will want to implement a survey on your confirmation page to try and gain as much information about your customers as possible.

Once you can start looking at the metrics of the people who are purchasing your products, you can start honing in on who purchases your products the most. Your goal should be to determine a general range of individuals most interested in your products and shift the majority of your marketing to targeting those groups.

Once you have a clear idea of who you want to target, with most of your marketing, you will want to determine how you are going to go about conveying to them what your unique selling point (USP) is. To do this you are going to want to start by making a list of all of the features that your products have and then cross off the ones that more than a single competitor can also offer. Don't forget to consider emotional needs that your product fills. Finally, you will want to clearly express the features and needs and spell them out on each product page.

Build your brand
Building your brand is an important part of ensuring your online store will see success in the long term. Building your brand is a culmination of many different elements including the colors of your store, the logo you choose to represent your store and the mission statement and ethics that your store represents.

When it comes to choosing the colors for your store, the first thing you should consider is a few core colors that complement one another as well as few more colors that are variations on the first. It is important to keep the color variation to a minimum as simple, clean looks are currently in fashion. Certain colors are also known to stimulate certain responses which make them natural choices when it comes to selling certain products.

Brown is known to reassure shoppers while also coming off as confident. Orange is an energetic color that radiates warmth, originality, passion and a fresh start, likewise, when it is paired with blue it will make the customer view the related content as new and exciting. Yellow is an attention grabbing color that is also playful as long as it is used in moderation; yellow that is too strong is known to decrease customer interest. Green is a positive color that conjures up harmony, safety, relaxation and positivity. Blue is peaceful, thoughtful and productive, but it should not be used if you are selling items related to food as it is known to decrease the appetite.

When it comes to designing a logo, it is important to consider what you ultimately go with long and hard as your logo is going to be seen more than any other aspect of your business. When it comes to finding the right logo for you, a good place to start is with common symbols as when done properly your logo will spring to mind whenever that symbol is used. When thinking about your logo it is important to consider how it looks when it is the size of a thumbnail as it is when it is filling your screen completely. You never know where your logo might end up and it is important to plan accordingly. Likewise, it is important to pick a logo that can default to colors that resemble the colors of your store but it should be just as recognizable when any other colors are inserted into the mix.

When choosing a logo, it is important to pick something that is timeless instead of cashing in on a current trend. While a trendy logo might get you some notice today, it is much more likely to be a hindrance in the long run. Create a logo that you are sure will be comfortable with for the foreseeable future.

When it comes to determining your mission statement and ethics there are several important things to try and cover. You will want to make it clear what the purpose of your company is in a way that can be inspirational to your customers. You will want to make it clear what values your company holds in the highest regard and how you plan to conduct business in a general sense. You should also make it clear how this goal directly benefits those who purchase your products.

Additionally, you will want to include any thoughts you have on the character of your business or any types of social or behavioral standards you are willing to promise to always try and uphold. It is important to create a mission statement that makes it clear what sets you apart from other similar stores, while at the same time not limiting your potential growth. While it is easy to start making promise to customers, it is important to keep yourself in check and only promise things that you know you can deliver on in both the short and the long term.

Consider Content Marketing
Especially when you are first starting your Shopify store, there are few ways of more effectively marketing your existence then doing everything in your power to be seen as an expert on the niche in question. This process can take a fair amount of work but the results will pay for themselves countless times over when done properly. To get started with content marketing you will want to take advantage of ability to build a blog on your Shopify page and then start filling it with content that your target audience will genuinely appreciate.

Create the type of content that your target audience considers both relevant and useful will serve several purposes. First, as the quality of your content becomes more widely known, it will drive traffic to your website that you can then potentially convert into sales. Indeed, every piece of content you create can be seen as a direct contribution to your marketing efforts. What's more, some of this content can be discussions of products that you are currently selling on your site as well as breakdowns of the specifics of each. These blog posts can then contain links to the sales page, closing the loop on customers who only look at the blog and never at the rest of the site.

In addition to directly driving customers, and sales depending, to your Shopify page, regularly generating content that your customers either find interesting or easy to relate to serves a larger purpose as well. This is to cement you as an expert in the niche in question which will then serve the added bonus of making any products you write about or recommend carry an added weight that being an expert conveys. When it comes to creating the type of well thought out and useful content that you will want to generate in order to create the image you are hoping to achieve the first thing you are going to want to do is some homework.

In this case it means really learning everything there is to know about a portion of the niche that your target audience is a part of. This means more than simply reading the related Wikipedia page, though that is a good place to start though only for the sources that are referenced at the bottom of the page. You are going to need to go deep if you are hoping for this type of marketing approach to be successful, as you are going to need to be able to generate new and relevant content on a regular basis if you hope to see any results on this front.

Once you are very familiar with your topic, the next step to being seen as an expert is to get your name out there in niche-specific circles. This means posting thoughtful comments to the subreddits related to your niche, popular social media destinations for your target audience and even on the blogs of other Shopify users who are dealing in the same niche. Your goal should be to make it so that your potential customers can't go anywhere in the digital world without seeing your name in relation to the products and your niche in question. Always include your logo in all of your comments as well as a link to your page when appropriate.

If you are looking for another easy way to make yourself appear as though you are an expert in the niche in question, one of the easiest ways is publishing as an eBook on the topic, and then displaying that book prominently on your Shopify page. As an added bonus, the book can be given away for free to stimulate email address collection for the email marketing tips described below. Publishing an eBook is as easy as going to UpWork.com or similar websites and looking for a ghostwriter whom you can often procure for around $1 per 100 words which means a hefty 12,000-word book like this one will run your around $120. From there around the same amount gets you a finished book that you can post to the Kindle Marketplace for free.

Consider Email Marketing

While public opinion has turned against email marketing in the last decade, the reality is that it is still the single most effective type of marketing that an online business can partake in. When done properly, email marketing is said to have a return on investment of nearly 4,000 percent.

When it comes to generating emails that your former customers are likely to open, you will again want to include the types of useful content that your target audience is sure to be interested in. You can even start blog posts on your blog and then finish them in your email marketing newsletter as a way of building a list of interested parties. When generating content, it is important to include enough sales material to ensure that you see a return on your investment, without making the entire newsletter nothing more than one long advertisement. When in doubt err on the side of too much useful content instead of not enough.

To create an effective email marketing strategy, the first thing you are going to want to do is determine just what your goals with email marketing are going to be. This will allow you to tailor your content in a way that generate the greatest amount of positive results in the shortest period of time. When it comes to generating goals, consider how much content you plan to create each week, how you will connect the email newsletter with sales, how you will attract new subscribers and how the email newsletter can tie into your broader marketing goals.

From there it is simply a matter of generating the right email newsletter list which can be easier said than done. The first thing you will need to do is create a new page on your site to link people to who are interested in signing up for your email newsletter. There should be a link to this page from your blog as well as on the order confirmation page that every customer sees after they have completed their order, these are the most valuable customers you have as they have already bought products from you once which makes them more likely to do so again in the future.

When it comes to attracting new email subscribers, the best way to do so is to promise access to something with a perceived value, say an eBook you had written, in exchange for signing up for your newsletter. It is important to not use underhanded tactics to get people to sign up for your newsletter or to gain their email address through other means and then send an unsolicited email. Either of these actions are only going to get your email marked as spam, they will never, ever get anyone to open them unsolicited.

Once you have a new subscriber, you will want to ensure they open the first email they receive from you by including the right subject line. The subject line is one of the only things that you can reliably assume your subscribers are going to see which makes it extremely important when it comes to influencing open rates. Surprisingly, studies show that the true determining factor as to whether an email will be opened is not the content of the subject line, but its length. This means that subject lines under 60 characters or over 70 character will likely see an average open rate, while those with a subject line of between 60 and 70 will see dramatically less. All told, less than 40 total characters tends to see the best results.

Additionally, you will want to time your weekly email newsletters to go out on Friday or Saturday night, after 9 pm. Studies show that the best time to capture subscribers' interest is to ensure they are likely to start interacting with your email first thing in the morning or on the weekends. In other words, the more time they have to interact with your content the better.

Cashing in on holidays
When it comes to preparing for holiday sales, discounts and deals are nice, but so is an optimized customer experience. This means it is important to check each of your product pages as well as your checkout services to ensure that everything is working as smoothly as possible on both your mobile site and your traditional site. Especially during the holiday rush, customers are in search of as many ways to make their lives easier as possible which means they are likely to bolt at the first sign of inconvenience.

Likewise, you are likely to see a much higher number of conversions if you offer a wider range of shipping options to facilitate those who are shopping at the last minute. Don't worry about the extravagant costs, people will pay them eventually. Additionally, you will see a higher number of conversions farther out from the actual holiday if you bite the bullet and eat the shipping costs for a specified period of time. Ensure your customers are aware of the timeframe and watch your sales soar.

While you may be tempted to lower your prices to grab a few extra customers, the strategy of offering deep discounts occasionally is actually less productive than you might think. For starters, around the holidays anyone who is looking for a present related to your niche is likely going to purchase your products anyway, that's the benefit of working in a niche. Second, while it will likely create a spike in sales in the short term, in the long term you are likely to notice a slightly lower overall sales rate because you have trained some of your customers to hold off making a purchase in hopes that you will drop the price on the item they have their eye on.

Paying for Advertising
Depending on the type of niche store you are selling, there are numerous types of advertising you should try before you begin to explore the options relating to paying for advertising. After that it will help to have a good idea of just what you can expect when it comes to various types of paid advertising.

Banner ads: Banner ads are the most common type of internet advertisements and they can be seen on everything from webpages to next to these very words if you are using a free third party eBook reader. These ads are extremely prevalent online to the point that many users ignore them entirely. They are useful if targeted properly, however and can be purchased on either a pay per visitor model or a pay per 1,000 views model. If you plan on using this type of advertising, you will want to have a very clear idea of just what your conversation rates from this advertising is.

Text advertising: This type of advertising is often found on Google search engine results and consists of just text and a link to your page. Depending on the niche in question this can be a valuable advertising tool if you can set your business apart from others in the same niche in just a few words.

Google AdWords: This type of advertising is often considered the most popular among those who own and operate an online store. Google offers text and display ads in relation to keywords or phrased that you specify. Additionally, the long that you pay for Google AdWords advertising, the higher your related quality score is going to be. Having a higher quality score makes it more likely that your advertising will appear when the targeted keywords are used.

Chapter 6: Expanding Your Product Line

Once you have finally gotten everything up and rolling there is nothing left to do but keep your nose to the grindstone and keeping marketing your store until you find success. Eventually you are going to feel the need to begin expanding the types of products that your store sells, and in doing so you will open yourself up to many new questions and concerns.

Adding products tactically
The life cycle of the products on your page can be seen as being in one of four primary cycles. The startup phase is when a product first comes on the market and you are building awareness of it. The second is growth when sales of that particular product are growing the most; this is followed by maturity when the product begins to regularly sell an expected amount of units. Finally, the maturity stage is then sometimes followed by the exit stage is when the interest for the product is in a decline. While not every product hits all the stages, when a product begins to decline in sales you need to know what to do.

When you are ready to start expanding your stock, what you need to do is look at the analytics and determine just which of your products are producing the most consistent conversions. From there, it is simply a matter of analyzing the data and determining if adding another similar item would likely split the number of sales or if it is likely to double them. If this does not appear to be a step in the right direction, instead it might be better to determine why interest has dropped off on the product in question. Many of the common reasons for a product's decline have to do with a newer version being released or a change in the practices related to how that product is made or used. If this is the case, then something as simple as a few minutes' research can totally refresh your product line.

Find out what your customers want by including a survey regarding a product expansion in an email newsletter. There is nothing to be gained by beating around the bush in this instance and, because only your best customers are likely going to interact with your newsletter, you have a way to directly ask your target audience what they want to buy from you. Take the time to draft up a realistic grouping of new products and also leave room for a write in section, you may be surprised at the results you find.

Finding new products
When it comes to looking for new products to sell, the first thing you are going to want to do is take a look at your existing stock and see if there are any obvious holes in your product line. If nothing sticks out to you at this point, your next best bet is likely to be to get offline and out into the world of brick and mortar retail stores. Take the time to seek out local variations on the theme of your niche and you might be surprised at how easily a new product idea or service comes to mind.

Back online, another viable alternative that more and more online stores are embracing is the world of Kickstarter manufacturers. Finding niche relevant content in this area is as easy as going to Kickstarter.com and looking through successfully funded Kickstarter pages to find products that might speak to your niche. Getting in touch with these types of manufacturers can often lead to a mutually beneficial relationship wherein they get a way to sell their product once they have delivered on their initial backer promises and you get an exclusive item that there is a proven demand for.

With that being said, it is important to ensure that the demand in question hasn't burned out with the fulfillment of the Kickstarter campaign, do some research and search out any additional demand or the product, the faster the better as if you don't meet the demand someone else will. While forming a good relationship with a Kickstarter manufacturer can lead to great things, it is important to do your research and only deal with manufacturers who have already successfully shipped product.

The great thing about Kickstarter is that anyone with an idea can get it funded, but this means that oftentimes people need to adapt to new roles on the fly which can be more difficult than it might first appear. Ensuring that the company has shipped product first will go a long way towards weeding out many of the problems inherent in the early days of a manufacturing company. Regardless, it is important to never offer to pay for exclusivity and to always get everything in writing as you will not be able to safely assume the company is not going to fold until they have sent you a few shipments of products.

Conclusion

Thank for making it through to the end of *Shopify: Beginner to Pro Seller – The Comprehensive Guide*, let's hope it was informative and was able to provide you with all of the tools you need to achieve your goals both in the near term and for the months and years ahead. Remember, just because you've finished this book doesn't mean there is nothing left to learn on the topic. Becoming an expert at something is a marathon, not a sprint, slow and steady wins the race.

The next step is to stop reading and start preparing to create the type of Shopify page that is sure to generate as many conversions as possible. It is important to not get so excited to proceed that you do so in a foolhardy fashion, however, take the time to determine the right niche, the right products, and the right style for your site before you go ahead and take things live. Remember, you only have one chance to make a first impression, you best make the most of it if you ever hope to fulfil your online business dreams.

Finally, if you found this book useful in anyway, a review on Amazon is always appreciated!

www.ingramcontent.com/pod-product-compliance
Lightning Source LLC
Chambersburg PA
CBHW070403190526
45169CB00003B/1096